How to Survive Being a

CAT OWNER

CLIVE WHICHELOW *and* **MIKE HASKINS**

summersdale

HOW TO SURVIVE BEING A CAT OWNER

Summersdale Publishers Ltd
46 West Street
Chichester
West Sussex
PO19 1RP
UK

www.summersdale.com

Printed and bound in China

ISBN: 978-1-78685-264-9

Substantial discounts on bulk quantities of Summersdale books are available to corporations, professional associations and other organisations. For details contact general enquiries: telephone: +44 (0) 1243 771107 or email: enquiries@summersdale.com.

To....................................

From................................

Introduction

What's so hard about owning a cat? They're cute, cuddly, furry, purry – what's not to like?

Well, where do we begin?

The thing about cats is that they lull you into a false sense of ease. If you get one as a kitten you can forgive its endearing little habits – such as ripping chunks out of your best cushions or making a mess on your prized Axminster – and pass them off as youthful indiscretions that they will grow out of.

What you forget in your enthusiasm for this lovely new little companion is that the blighters can't be trained. Was there ever a popular TV series called *One Man and His Cat*? Has there ever been a brilliant performing cat act on *Britain's Got Talent*? Do they have guide cats for the blind, police mogs, sniffer cats?

The answer to all these questions is no. Cats are untrainable. They are masters and mistresses of their own destiny. They do their own thing. And boy, do they do it! Whether it's dragging dead birds through the cat flap, snaffling your lunchtime tuna salad off the kitchen worktop or using your dining-room chairs as handy scratching posts, they will find 101 ways of getting your goat.

Of course, they're lovely, and we wouldn't be without them, but at times they will test your patience to the limit and leave it wanting.

So, here, at last, is what cat owners everywhere have been waiting for: the ultimate guide to surviving being a cat owner. Purr-use it at your leisure!

THE UPSIDES AND DOWNSIDES
OF OWNING A CAT

UPSIDE	DOWNSIDE
They are very independent	But this doesn't mean that they go to the supermarket to buy their own cat food
They show their affection by rubbing round your ankles	Unfortunately, they often do this while you are walking down the stairs, half asleep
They are clean and hygienic and take care to bury their poo	You will find cat poo hidden in all sorts of unexpected locations throughout your garden and home
They like to sit contentedly purring on your knee	If you make a move, they will dig their claws into your legs to stop you

TYPES OF CAT OWNER YOU COULD BE

Soft, soppy, indulgent – just the sort of human a conniving cat likes!

. . . .

One who treats the cat like a child – and ends up with a teenage delinquent!

. . . .

Insatiable – continually acquiring more and more cats until no surface in your house is left unoccupied by a cat and you have nowhere to sit down

THE COOL
PROFESSIONAL – HAS
A HIGH-PROFILE JOB
IN THE CITY AND LIVES
ALONE IN A STYLISH
FLAT WITH A CAT WHICH
ALSO LOOKS LIKE IT HAS
A HIGH-PROFILE JOB
IN THE CITY

TYPES OF CAT YOUR CAT COULD BE

Irritatingly indecisive – miaows to be let out before, five minutes later, miaowing to be let back in again

. . . .

Not a people-pleaser – refuses to play with the ball of paper you keep dangling in front of it

. . . .

Split personality – purrs contentedly while being stroked then suddenly goes for you with teeth bared and claws flailing

The daredevil – compelled to scale the tallest objects in the vicinity and walk along the highest, narrowest ledges it can find

A BREAKDOWN OF HOW YOU WILL SPEND YOUR TIME AS A CAT OWNER

Going round taking the posters down because you found your cat asleep in a drawer
9%

Feeding the cat
9%

Buying more cat food
9%

Going round the neighbourhood putting up posters because your cat is missing
9%

Chasing it away from places it shouldn't be
10%

Standing at door calling cat's name
9%

Letting it in the house
9%

Letting it out of the house
9%

Waiting at the vet's
9%

Trying to get the cat into the carrier to go to the vet
9%

Letting it back in again
9%

GADGETS A CAT OWNER MAY NEED

A special hooked stick for getting
fur balls out of the cat's throat

. . . .

A tracking device so you don't end up
out of your mind with worry when the cat
decides to wander off for a couple of days

. . . .

An alarm that will start bleeping if your
home begins reeking too much of cat food

A tiny medical
emergency kit including
a defibrillator to revive
all the small creatures
brought home by your cat

WHAT YOUR CAT THINKS OF THE THINGS YOU DO

WHAT YOU DO	WHAT YOUR CAT THINKS
You sit on your favourite chair	You're sitting on her favourite chair
You drop a ball of wool on the floor	You've just given him a new toy
You enter the kitchen	The only imaginable reason you have done this is because you're about to dish out an orgiastic feast for them
You buy a brand new three-piece furniture suite	You have bought a brand new three-piece set of scratching posts

HOW CATS COMMUNICATE WITH OTHER CATS

They make an eerie low growling sound
– other cats know that this is done
purely to wind up their owners who
think a massive fight is about to start

. . . .

They go and make a mess in another cat's
garden just to show them who's boss

. . . .

They hiss at each other as though they are
attending a pantomime and a moustache-
twirling villain has just walked on stage

Their fur all stands up on end, either to try to make themselves look bigger or in order to look like a punk rocker with spiked-up hair

CAT BEHAVIOUR
THAT NON-CAT OWNERS MIGHT FIND WORRYING

Suddenly running between your legs – usually when you're carrying a tray of hot tea or walking down the stairs

Climbing onto roofs – are they planning to jump onto your head?

. . . .

Leaping into your face out of a drawer as it's opened – you've disturbed them from the nice cosy spot they found to snuggle down in

. . . .

Looking like they've just seen something terrifying – have they seen a ghost or are they just doing it to wind you up?

THINGS THAT ONLY CAT OWNERS HAVE TO PUT UP WITH

In the middle of the night the cat suddenly realises that your bed is far more comfortable than their own

• • • • • • • • • •

When you're in the middle of an important email, your cat settles down on your computer keyboard

• • • • • • • • • •

Knowing that when Aunt Mabel comes for tea, the cat will give its bottom a thorough clean right in front of her

Out of the blue they decide they don't like the cat food you've been serving them for the previous 15 years

HOW TO CONVINCE PEOPLE THAT YOUR CAT IS FRIENDLY

Insist that the manic swishing of its tail is merely its way of keeping cool

. . . .

Tell them he isn't growling at them, he's just doing his impersonation of a dog

. . . .

Say that she only hisses because she wants to come closer to whisper a little secret in your ear

Say that he only bites
people he likes

NAMES YOU SHOULDN'T CALL YOUR CAT

%!$!! – even if they have just dug up your prized petunias

. . . .

Fire – it could alarm the neighbours when you call him in at night

. . . .

Pussy – you don't want to be heard shouting this from your door in an increasing state of desperation

LUCKY – NAMING YOUR CAT THIS IS SURELY TEMPTING FATE TO DO ITS WORST TO THE POOR CREATURE

REALISTIC AND UNREALISTIC GOALS FOR YOUR CAT

REALISTIC	UNREALISTIC
They will become part of your family	They will start doing their own washing up
They will be admired by friends and visitors	They will become a YouTube sensation and earn you millions in merchandising rights
They will provide companionship	You will start going out on double dates together
They will lower your heart rate and be good for your health	If anything happens to you, they will dial 999

THINGS NON-CAT OWNERS DON'T UNDERSTAND ABOUT CATS

It's the cat's house – you just happen to live there too

. . . .

Cats do not understand the use of tense in the phrase 'I will feed you in a minute'

. . . .

You do not just have to stroke cats for a few minutes, you have to keep stroking them all the time while you are in their presence or suffer a vicious attack

WAYS A CAT WILL CHANGE THE APPEARANCE OF YOUR HOUSE

Your paintwork will have that fashionably 'distressed' look whether you like it or not

. . . .

Your soft furnishings will all be torn and have pulled threads up to the point that your cat can reach

. . . .

The floorboards throughout your house will gradually accumulate a layer of fur as though they are growing a carpet

Your garden will now be full of old CDs because you've been told it keeps the cats off your plants

WAYS IN WHICH
YOUR CAT WILL
CHANGE YOU

Without noticing it, you will gradually build up a large collection of cat mugs, coasters, tea towels and other cat-related items that people have given you as presents

You will have to make sure your holidays don't clash with those of the people who who you have a mutual cat-feeding arrangement with

. . . .

You will become immune to unimaginable odours and be happy to live in a house that smells like a fish-gutting factory

. . . .

You will be the equivalent of a black belt in being able to squeeze a wild, hissing feline into a carrier to go to the vet

BREAKDOWN OF A CAT'S DAY

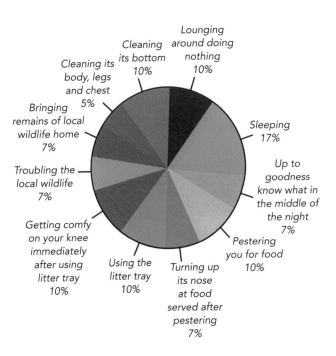

Cleaning its bottom
10%

Lounging around doing nothing
10%

Cleaning its body, legs and chest
5%

Bringing remains of local wildlife home
7%

Troubling the local wildlife
7%

Getting comfy on your knee immediately after using litter tray
10%

Using the litter tray
10%

Turning up its nose at food served after pestering
7%

Pestering you for food
10%

Up to goodness know what in the middle of the night
7%

Sleeping
17%

GOOD AND BAD THINGS ABOUT CAT FOOD

GOOD	BAD
Those little sachets are very convenient	You can never quite get the last bit out
They now do all sorts of posh gourmet versions	Once your cat has had a taste of those you'll never get them back on the cheap stuff
Sometimes the posh gourmet foods are available at a special reduced price	Your cat will somehow be aware of such offers and will refuse to eat this food as soon as you stock up with a few months' supply
Dry, relatively odourless varieties are available	These will be converted in your cat's stomach to something moist and smelly before being brought back up and left in various locations around your house

THINGS YOUR CAT WILL BRING IN AND WHAT TO DO WITH THEM

Live mice – you will be torn between freeing the mouse and allowing it to run around your house, or leaving the cat to do what comes naturally

. . . .

Parts of creatures – you can conduct a forensic investigation and reconstruct the small creature that has met its unhappy end (the culprit responsible will, however, already be known to you)

. . . .

Fleas – the one creature your cat is likely to bring home alive and thriving

Dead mice – give them a dignified burial in the garden and hope your cat doesn't dig them up again

THOUGHTS ABOUT YOUR CAT THAT WILL CAUSE YOU UNNECESSARY STRESS

Your cat is ageing at four times the rate that you are, but still seems far healthier than you

. . . .

If your cat ever learns how to use a tin-opener or open a sachet on its own, you can pack your bags

. . . .

Your cat might get lost and not be able to find its way home – even worse, she might find her way into a neighbour's house and find it preferable to yours

THINGS ONLY A CAT OWNER WOULD FIND EXCITING

A fabulous new website called
catsdothecraziestthings.com

. . . .

The latest developments in
flea-treatment products

. . . .

Seeing another cat who looks a
little bit similar to your cat

Cat Crunchies in a
brand-new shape

PET FOOD
CAT CRUNCHIES NEW- STAR SHAPED!
CAT CRUNCHIES NEW- STAR SHAPED!

APPROPRIATE AND INAPPROPRIATE TOYS FOR CATS

APPROPRIATE	INAPPROPRIATE
A scrunched-up ball of paper	A scrunched-up copy of your tax return
A wind-up toy mouse to chase around	A real mouse that you regularly have to replace when the cat catches it
A small toy attached to a piece of string or elastic	Attaching the cat itself to a piece of string or elastic
A soft toy impregnated with catnip which will either drive your cat wild or calm it right down	A soft toy impregnated with morphine to really make your cat zone out

That your cat can actually understand what you are saying and may soon even start speaking itself

. . . .

That you'll be reincarnated as a cat and spend most of your life lounging around and being waited on hand and foot

. . . .

That you get shrunk down to the size of a mouse and find out how much love your cat still has for you then

That your cat takes his revenge by putting you in to a big cage and taking you to the vet to be operated on against your will

'They "know" when you're planning
on taking them to the vet's'

. . . .

'Don't worry, if they fall off the roof
they will always land on their feet'

. . . .

'It is possible to train your
cat to be a vegetarian'

. . . .

'Don't worry! Cat fleas aren't
interested in biting humans'

HABITS THAT MAY SUGGEST YOU ARE TOO SUBSERVIENT TO YOUR CAT

When she's sitting on 'your' chair you go to sit on another one without a murmur

. . . .

Your cat has learnt to shake the little bell on his collar to summon you

. . . .

Your choice of (human) life partner depends on whether the cat likes them or not

Your cat not only has its own armchair but also its own TV remote control

WAYS IN WHICH HAVING A CAT IS BETTER THAN HAVING A PARTNER

When cats sleep on your bed
they don't hog the duvet

. . . .

They can keep themselves clean without
taking up the bathroom for hours and
running up excessive utility bills

. . . .

If you're not sure where they've gone,
you don't need to text or call – you can
just stand at the door shaking a box
of dried food until they reappear

WAYS IN WHICH ADVERTS FOR CAT FOOD GET IT WRONG

In adverts the cat never turns its nose up
at what's served and walks off in a huff

. . . .

The owner depicted in the ad very rarely
grimaces in disgust after opening the sachet

. . . .

The cat never brings its dinner up
straight after eating only to see it
swiftly consumed by the dog

Your cat doesn't usually do astonishing acrobatic tricks to get your attention for food

HOW PEOPLE WILL BE ABLE TO TELL YOU ARE A CAT OWNER

There is more cat food than human food in your supermarket basket

· · · · · · · · · · ·

Collectively, your clothes are covered in almost as much cat hair as the cat itself

YOUR MUG AT WORK,
YOUR KEY FOB,
TEA TOWELS AND
COUNTLESS OTHER
PERSONAL ITEMS
ARE FESTOONED
WITH IMAGES OF
CUTE CATS

You are covered in scratches from playing with your cat

APPROPRIATE AND INAPPROPRIATE TREATS FOR CATS

APPROPRIATE	INAPPROPRIATE
The leftover fish in the bottom of the tin	The leftover fish in white wine sauce that you have brought home from a posh restaurant
A piece of the turkey at Christmas	Their own special Christmas dinner with all the trimmings and a party hat
A few pieces of fresh chicken	Being left in charge of the hen house in your back garden
A bag of specially made tasty cat treats from the supermarket	Their own individual store account and supermarket loyalty card

'Does he sleep *all* the time?'
'No, he gets up just after we've gone
to bed and miaows to be let out!'

. . . .

'She only brings mice in as a
"little present" for you.'
'I know, I keep telling her I'd prefer a box
of chocolates but she won't listen!'

. . . .

'Do you see your cat as a
substitute for a child?'
'No, but I do think of children as
being substitutes for cats!'

'Is talking to your cat the first sign of madness?'
'No – it's the first sign of finding someone who actually listens to me!'

THINGS IT IS UNLIKELY YOU WILL BE ABLE TO GET YOUR CAT TO DO

Jump happily into the carrying
basket to go to the vet's

. . . .

Eat the 'basic' range of cat food from
your local budget supermarket

. . . .

Clean its feet between moving
from the litter tray to your lap

. . . .

Take an interest in local bird and
small animal conservation

THE IDEAL CAT vs YOUR CAT

IDEAL CAT	YOUR CAT
Adds to the cosy scene at Christmas by snuggling down in front of your beautifully decorated tree	Crampons its way through the tinsel in pursuit of a glittering bauble only to bring the whole tree crashing down
Jumps onto your lap while you're watching TV and purrs contentedly	Jumps on your TV dinner while you're not looking and tries to scoff it
Always waiting for you when you open the door	Always waiting to attack you as soon as you open the door
Settles down on your lap when you're sitting reading the paper	Clamps itself to your lap with its claws even when you stand up and walk away

HOW TO UNDERSTAND WHAT YOUR CAT IS TRYING TO TELL YOU

An accusing stare – you are sitting in his favourite chair

A blood-curdling yowl that makes
you jump out of your skin –
you're standing on her tail

. . . .

Miaowing and brushing past
your legs – 'Feed me!'

. . . .

Pacing back and forth and
getting under your feet –
'Feed me some more!'

FAMOUS CATS AND WHY YOURS ISN'T LIKE THEM

Garfield – despite being extremely lazy he still manages to make millions of dollars every year

. . . .

The Cat in the Hat – like your cat he makes a mess, but unlike your cat he cleans up afterwards

. . . .

Top Cat – he's better dressed than your cat – or at least he is from the waist upwards

CATS ON THE
INTERNET — ALWAYS
ADORABLE TO WATCH
BUT, UNLIKE YOUR
MOGGY, THESE ONES
CAN BE SWITCHED
OFF WHEN YOU GET
TIRED OF THEM

GOOD AND BAD REASONS FOR TAKING YOUR CAT TO THE VET

GOOD REASONS	BAD REASONS
You've noticed they haven't eaten for a couple of days	You've noticed that they haven't eaten the cheaper cat food you've been trying to palm them off with
You've noticed them limping	You think it's time you got your money's worth out of that expensive pet insurance
You've noticed he is sleeping a lot	You want the vet to make him sleep a lot more
You've noticed she has recently become very smelly	You want to disperse the smell away from your house and into the vet's

YOUR FINANCIAL OUTGOINGS FROM NOW ON

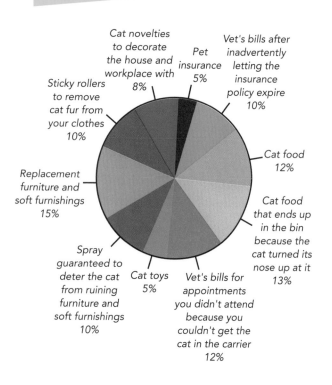

Cat novelties to decorate the house and workplace with
8%

Pet insurance
5%

Vet's bills after inadvertently letting the insurance policy expire
10%

Sticky rollers to remove cat fur from your clothes
10%

Replacement furniture and soft furnishings
15%

Cat food
12%

Cat food that ends up in the bin because the cat turned its nose up at it
13%

Spray guaranteed to deter the cat from ruining furniture and soft furnishings
10%

Cat toys
5%

Vet's bills for appointments you didn't attend because you couldn't get the cat in the carrier
12%

WAYS YOUR CAT MAY RESIST BEING GIVEN MEDICATION

By steadfastly refusing to open its
mouth and emitting a low growl

. . . .

Spitting out the tablet you have
cunningly hidden in its dish of food

. . . .

Attacking you viciously every time you try
to slip the pill back into the food bowl

By scuttling through the cat flap as soon as it spots you reaching for the pill bottle

A GUIDE TO THE ITEMS THAT A CAT OWNER WILL HAVE IN THEIR LIVING ROOM

One extremely hairy armchair

. . . .

A pristine cat toy that the cat
resolutely refuses to play with

. . . .

A fluffy cat bed which attaches
to the radiator (again: not
investigated to date by the cat)

THINGS YOUR CAT WILL DO THAT RESULT IN YOU HAVING TO MAKE A DOCTOR'S APPOINTMENT

Bite your finger as you try to
pop a pill into its mouth

. . . .

Run between your legs as you step out
of the shower onto a slippery floor

. . . .

Launch itself at you, squealing like a
banshee, after being unexpectedly
disturbed thereby giving you a heart attack

Sleeping, unnoticed,
halfway down the stairs

SELF-HELP BOOKS YOU MIGHT WANT TO READ

Warning Signs That Your Cat is Becoming the Boss in Your Relationship

· · · · · · · · · · ·

Cat Psychology: Or How to Outwit Your Cat

· · · · · · · · · · ·

Hand to Claw Combat: A Beginner's Guide

· · · · · · · · · · ·

How to Make a Million with Your Cat: YouTube Edition

LIFESTYLE CHANGES NOW THAT YOU HAVE A CAT

You can't have an impromptu night away without making complicated cat-sitting arrangements

. . . .

You will no longer be able to make friends with people who are allergic to cats for fear of endangering their health

. . . .

Your neighbours will all have keys to get in and feed the cat while you're away and will have taken the opportunity to explore every room in your house

It is no longer safe to leave the table halfway through a meal

DOs AND DON'Ts WHEN LEAVING YOUR CAT TO GO ON HOLIDAY

DO	DON'T
Ask your neighbour to feed them	Send the cat postcards asking if 'that naughty neighbour' has remembered to feed it
Lock any rooms that you don't want the cat to get into	Install CCTV to check whether the cat has somehow breached your security system
Leave the vet's phone number in case your neighbour notices anything wrong with your cat while you're away	Leave a DIY guide to animal surgery in case your neighbour notices anything wrong with your cat while you're away
Book your cat into a luxury cat hotel while you're away	Nail the cat flap firmly shut and tell your cat to make its own arrangements

THE WORST THINGS YOUR CAT WILL DO AND HOW TO LOOK AT THEM POSITIVELY

Claw holes in your best curtains
– at least it wasn't your legs

. . . .

Two-timing you by deciding to move
in with a neighbour – it'll return
when you next get a special offer
coupon for his favourite cat food

. . . .

Using your pot plants as a litter tray
– it could be worse; it could have
been your shoes, hat or duvet

BRING HOME DEAD
MICE — BETTER
THAN BRINGING
HOME LIVE MICE

THINGS TO KEEP
TELLING YOURSELF

Cat owners live longer than non-cat owners
– it's probably all that exercise chasing
them off your newly planted flowerbeds

. . . .

You'll never find a more loyal companion
– at least not as long as you're feeding it

. . . .

You don't have to take it out for
walks – although you may have to
wander the streets for hours trying
to find where it has got to

Having a cat reduces
your heart rate –
although maybe not
when it jumps onto the
mantelpiece and decides
to slalom round your
priceless ornaments

THINGS YOUR CAT MIGHT ASK OF A GENIE

To make you their pet and
let you see how it feels

Three fishes

. . . .

For every dog it encounters to be tied
up on a lead just too short to reach it

. . . .

To be treated like royalty, to lie around
doing nothing all day and to have their own
personal servant who feeds them, attends
to their needs and massages them several
times a day... Wait a minute! It looks like the
cat's wishes have already been granted!

If you're interested in finding out more about our books, find us on Facebook at Summersdale Publishers and follow us on Twitter at @Summersdale.

www.summersdale.com